Voices of Women:

3 critics on 3 poets on 3 heroines

**Martha Kearns
Diane Radycki
May Stevens**

**Muriel Rukeyser
Adrienne Rich
Jane Cooper**

**Käthe Kollwitz
Paula Modersohn-Becker
Rosa Luxemburg**

with
an introductory essay
by
Lucy R. Lippard

MIDMARCH ARTS PRESS
New York   *1990*

MIDMARCH ARTS BOOKS

Artists and Their Cats
The Lady Architects:
Lois Lilley Howe, Eleanor Manning and Mary Almy, 1893-1937
Camera Fiends and Kodak Girls: 50 Selections by and about Women in
Photography 1840-1930
Yesterday and Tomorrow: California Women Artists
No Bluebonnets, No Yellow Roses: Texas Women in the Arts
Pilgrims and Pioneers: New England Women in the Arts
Whole Arts Directory
Women Artists of the World
Voices of Women: 3 critics on 3 poets on 3 heroines
American Women Artists: Works on Paper
Guide to Women's Art Organizations and Directory for the Arts

Second Printing 1990

Library of Congress Catalog Card Number: 80-80281
ISBN: 0-9602476-1-0

Copies of this book may be obtained from:
Midmarch Arts Books
Box 3304 Grand Central Station
New York, NY 10163

Reissue of this publication has been made possible through the support of Lioness Books.

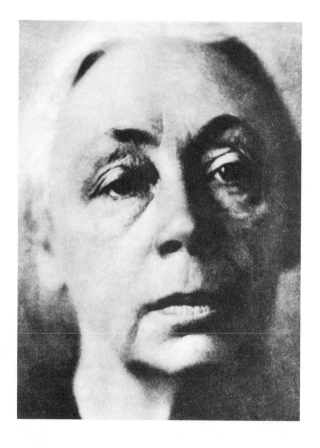

Käthe Kollwitz, photograph by Lotte Jacobi (signed)

Contents

Käthe Kollwitz: *Memorial for Karl Liebknecht,* woodcut, 1919

To the Third Power:
Art and Writing and Social Change
by Lucy R. Lippard

Making poetry out of politics, making art from lives lived outside of power, and making politics out of that art and poetry—
these are the three solid dimensions, the third power of the
women's liberation movement. Without any one of these ele-
ments, feminism is not whole. The women in this book, lone-
ly in their courageous confrontation of this fact, look to other
women for support. The "first generation" looks to friends—
painter Paula Modersohn-Becker to sculptor Clara Westhoff;
sculptor Käthe Kollwitz to herself, in diaries; theoretician
Rosa Luxemburg to Sophie Liebknecht, wife of the man with
whom she was to be assassinated. The second generation
looks back to artists in mediums other than their own—poet
Rich to painter Becker, poet Rukeyser to sculptor Kollwitz,
poet Cooper to activist Luxemburg. And finally the third
"tier" (also in the second generation)—the scholars and com-
mentators, art historians Radycki and Kearns and painter
Stevens—seeking the meaning of these pairings. In Stevens'
case there is yet another level—the blending of images and
words in her own collaged homages to Rosa Luxemburg,
which compare the "extraordinary life" of a brilliant political
activist to the "ordinary" life of her own mother—equally
tragic and significant in its own way.

Three layers is probably enough; a fourth, from me, is
merely icing. The book's internal richness—the lines cast out
in so many directions—speaks for itself. It also speaks for the
ways in which silences have been broken in this century.
Along with Tillie Olsen and Adrienne Rich, we are still naming
those silences and still understanding the ways in which they
fed each other, how women like Becker, Kollwitz, and Luxemburg sustained their words, their forms, their ideas, beneath
the weight of those silences. "Women as gates," says Rukeyser.

Each public gesture is a gate to another woman whose experience may coincide with or never approach ours. These gates, however, are often left closed. Here they are flung open, welcoming us as readers to lives we never could have lived and, at the same time, lives that offer models for the way we'd like to live. Kollwitz and Luxemburg were revolutionaries, the one an artist who understood politics, the other a political person who understood the arts. Becker's wars took place on a domestic battlefield and on her canvases, but hers too was a kind of revolution, illuminated by her letters. I don't see how anyone reading the three poems included here could resist going directly to the diaries and the letters themselves. The poems and collages join and distill events, years, feelings into a single form. Yet they don't synopsize. They bridge the gap. They remove, in a sense, the invisible third person to whom the sources were addressed and make us, the present readers, into the confidantes.

We are so used to reading about visual artists in the dry prose of the uninvolved that it is wonderful to hear other artists entering the chorus, taking images and physical facts in their own hands and molding a new kind of art from the original one. The threads that bind the arts together and the analyses that bring to the surface the meaning of those arts are still new enough to women's work that we rejoice every time one appears. This book is another step in freeing us from the alienation of women from history. "Which of us, Clara, hasn't had to take that leap / out beyond our being women / to save our work? or is it to save ourselves? / Marriage is lonelier than solitude," writes Rich with Becker. (And which of us has not thought these words as we struggled with the multiple roles that oppress and broaden us?) "Held between wars / my lifetime / among wars, the big hands of the world of death," writes Rukeyser with Kollwitz; "We live in the painfulest moment of evolution, the very chapter of change," says Cooper with Luxemburg. (And which of us has not thought these words about our own times?)

Finally, it is the relationship between the first two generations, between the real-life source materials and the poems molded from them, that fascinates me most, that is so important for contemporary feminism. The third step—commentary, analysis, appreciation, homage—is necessary and straightforward; it in-forms, tells us what is fact and what is fiction and how and why the two are merged. Yet the first two operate in that crucial area opened up by feminist consciousness—the process by which the personal becomes public becomes political. Here, indeed, is the esthetic of the "ordinary and the extraordinary." A woman writes in her diary or to a friend; whoever she is, the letter form tends to be relatively relaxed and intimate. Another generation of women, moved by these initial conversations, comes along and transforms one already strong and poignant form into another, into "art." And then this art is offered to the world and, if it is effective, it is transformed once again into an instrument of social awareness and change.

For over a decade now, we have been questioning the conventional boundaries between life, art, and theory—or politics, art, and life. We have been denying the existence of class walls raised by the dominant culture, or leaping over them, or trying to blow them up. Yet there are differences between these three places from which our breath comes—life, art, and politics—and this book illuminates them. The three aspects answer different needs—the need to exist, the need to express the meaning of that existence, and the need to frame that existence in a way that is just and equally responsible to all people. At the same time, while the needs differ, there is no reason to conclude that they can't co-exist in the same person.

This is what is so moving about a great deal of art by women—its refusal to deny any part for the whole. For this reason collage has become a peculiarly female medium—not only because it provides a way of knitting the fragments of our lives together, but also because it leaves nothing out; it allows all three levels to confront each other without any one overpowering the other. Every piece in this book is in a sense a collage (and a "femmage"—the feminist alternative to "hommage" invented by painters Miriam Schapiro and Melissa Meyer). Each element reconciles at least two others—past and present, friend and friend, writer and reader, "found" and "imagined" materials, images and words. I hope it is the first of many such books in which women meet across the "disciplines," climb the stone walls between the fields, and, in a kind of esthetic parthenogenesis, fertilize each other as the earth goddess once created herself within herself, every year. Such a hope does not exclude the rest of the world, the economic struggle for dignity and peace. On the contrary, only when the two viewpoints meet will our goals be met. Becker, Kollwitz, Luxemburg, Rich, Rukeyser, Cooper, Radycki, Kearns, and Stevens know this.

6   Käthe Kollwitz: *Self-Portrait,* drawing, 1890

Martha Kearns
on
Muriel Rukeyser
on
Käthe Kollwitz

Muriel Rukeyser's exquisite poem, "Käthe Kollwitz," had a vital and pivotal influence on me when I was gathering material for the first biography of Kollwitz in English.[1] I had found only two sources of material that illuminated Kollwitz the woman: the primary source was Kollwitz' *Diaries and Letters;*[2] the second was the memoir of her lifelong best friend, Beate Bonus Jeep.[3] Rukeyser's poem "Käthe Kollwitz" not only contributed new psychological and artistic insights into Kollwitz but also affirmed, through the poet's voice, the need for a woman-oriented perspective on Kollwitz' life and *oeuvre*. The poet's passion for Kollwitz simultaneously pleads for and offers an understanding of her as an artist, a mother, and a personality deeply affected and artistically motivated by human suffering.

Before I read "Käthe Kollwitz," I had been stunned and disheartened by the lack of existing critical reference to the many women's issues implicit in Kollwitz' life and work. Three biases had contributed to the exclusion of Kollwitz' work from the critical attention, acclaim, and scholarship it warrants. The primary prejudice was that of male sexism: as a woman Kollwitz did not fit into art history's "mainstream" current of art—that is, the handful of so-called "great" men. Male scholars have created the esthetic criteria for inclusion, while misogynist social mores have reinforced those criteria. In addition, Kollwitz' medium—primarily the graphic arts— was considered by these historians to be of lesser artistic merit, scale, and monetary value than the "fine arts" of painting, sculpture, and architecture. Finally, Kollwitz' subjects—the worker, especially the working woman, and her portrayal of the mother as an heroic figure—were regarded as themes not appropriate for high art, a view that until very recently discouraged serious examination of this original and pioneering approach.

Rukeyser's poem, on the other hand, spoke with a genuine appreciation of the soul—the *woman's* soul—of the artist. In 1971, unlike today, there were few literary and academic books containing rigorous feminist perspectives and analyses. In contrast, Rukeyser's elegiac portrait demonstrated the usefulness of approaching the artist and her work from a woman's point of view.

Respect for Kollwitz as a woman is implicit in the poem. In addition, Rukeyser points to the blindness of sexism as the reason Kollwitz' work has been underrated. In a short, beautifully crafted juxtaposition of the male and female voices, Rukeyser dramatically shows that it has been male condescension, not a lack of artistic merit, that has relegated Kollwitz' *oeuvre* to an inferior status. A message repeated throughout the poem is that women share an experiential knowledge of common womanhood that transcends seemingly insurmountable barriers of time, country, and language. Although they have never formally met, they "know" one another. For the woman poet who is invoking the artist as muse, it is part of her task to "name" this knowing in her poem.

The poem yearns and exalts in the voice of the woman artist; the poet's voice grows in power and in self-appreciation as it reveals the artist's voice. Interestingly, the dominant voice of the poem, that of the woman artist, encompasses both poet and artist. In some passages Kollwitz is not present as the poet's muse but as herself; in others, the artist's words are restated in the voice of the poet, which distills their meaning and divines their import. In still other passages Kollwitz functions as the poet's *compañera* activist, and as her sister in motherhood.

In the first stanza of part I, the poet invokes the artist as muse, intoning Kollwitz' influence not only as an artist, but as a wise spirit: "my lifetime . . . among wars . . . listens to yours." In the next stanza, the poet personifies Kollwitz "in dailiness," embellishing the artist's famous imagery of finely sculpted, over-large hands. The last word in this section, the ambiguous "you," stands for the subject summoned but yet unknown: the woman artist.

In part II, the voice of the woman artist is enriched by a shifting back and forth between the personalities of Rukeyser and Kollwitz. The poet uses the theme of music to illustrate the overlapping, different aspects of the artist's personality as well as to introduce one of the subtle, very successful designs of the poem: the "interweave" of the voices of poet and artist. It is the sensibility of the woman and artist in which the poet is interested. In part II the poet incorporates the artist's voice into her own. Although the quotes are taken from a wide variety of Kollwitz' writings, revealing the complexity of her personality, all respond, directly or obliquely, to the poet's central question: What did it mean for you, Kollwitz, to be a woman artist?

The only male voice comes into play at the end of this section. In a very short, abrupt, and clean change of voice and place, the poet juxtaposes her own deep appreciation of the woman and artist—developed in the previous segments— with a sharp, one-line put-down by a man. The effect of his comment is dramatic and startling, as if he were not only speaking for himself, but were in fact the voice of Man passing judgment. Thus at the end of the section the poet removes us from the intimacy of Kollwitz' introspective thoughts and completes the thematic query by answering it in the public sphere: to be a woman artist meant that sexism would prevent people from perceiving her work's timeless worth.

Throughout part III, the voice is Rukeyser's; after hearing and echoing the artist's voice, the poet shifts to her own. The poet, in reverie, imagines the artist *in situ*—in the context of her life, the forger of her art—against a backdrop of a people ravaged by two world wars. The earlier imagery of "great hands" now informs the theme of "woman as gates": another Peter killed in another war; firestorm; / dark, light, as two hands, / this pole and that pole as the gates." This intricately wrought stanza reads as a poetic metaphor for the work of Kollwitz; like it, it stands as a passionate, artistically fine transformation of reality, ending with these immortal lines:

What would happen if one woman told the truth about her life? The world would split open

In the final two sections, the voice is Rukeyser's. Part IV describes the artist in three stages of physical and spiritual development: as a girl, as the mother bearing two sons, and as an old woman facing the challenge of her own death as well as that of her younger son. In the last stanza the poet alludes to the tragic muse of Kollwitz' creative impulse, but deftly changes it to refer to the task Kollwitz faced as mother, artist, and mortal. It is the death of her younger son, Peter, in World War I that summons her to make her son live through the beauty and passion of an artistic work. In the long, often frightening process of coming to terms with this personal trial through the permanence of sculpture, Kollwitz attained maturity and magnanimity as an artist. The poet's reference to this heroic struggle in the last stanza is sublime; rhythm and meaning are unified through the weighted, heavy beat of mostly one-syllable words that perfectly and almost unconsciously express the burden of the task: "wrestle with grief with time / from the material make / an art harder than bronze."

Part V completes the literary portrait. The conclusion, "Self-Portrait," completes the poet's stylistic and thematic development of the interweave of voices by intertwining the images of Kollwitz' self-portraits from ages fourteen to seventy-five. Rukeyser depicts the artist *as woman* with wisdom, courage, sensitivity, and compassion. She eulogizes Kollwitz as woman and as mother, then conceptualizes both these aspects as representative not only of every woman but of everyone—"the face of our age." The last lines end with an appropriate softness, due to a repetitive and careful use of words containing o's and soft consonants. In this final interweave of image and meaning, the woman artist is seen as one whose life and work profoundly affect each other. The visual art of Kollwitz and the literary art of Rukeyser are themselves not merely creative works but products of lives passionately lived.

Martha Kearns

---

[1] Martha Kearns, *Käthe Kollwitz: Woman and Artist;* Old Westbury, NY: The Feminist Press, 1976, 1977. Because of its literary and research significance, Muriel Rukeyser's poem "Käthe Kollwitz" is included as the epilogue.

[2] To date five books feature the writing of Kollwitz; however, all these have been edited extensively, not by Kollwitz, for publication. The definitive source, *Tagebuchblätter (Diaries),* eleven handwritten volumes, is in the Käthe Kollwitz-Archiv, Akademie der Künste, West Berlin. It should be noted that Kollwitz' prose shows a fine respect for literary style as well as for emotional and intellectual self-expression.

[3] Beate Bonus Jeep, *Sechzig Jahre Freundschaft mit Käthe Kollwitz (Sixty Years of Friendship with Käthe Kollwitz);* Berlin: Boppard, Karl Rauch Verlag, 1948. A personal account of the two women's lives from 1885 to 1945; as social history, it is especially valuable in its material on women art students in Berlin and Munich from 1885 to 1891.

12 Käthe Kollwitz: *Self-Portrait*, etching, 1910

Käthe Kollwitz
by Muriel Rukeyser

I

Held between wars
my lifetime
               among wars, the big hands of the world of death
my lifetime
listens to yours.

The faces of the sufferers
in the street, in dailiness,
their lives showing
through their bodies
a look as of music
the revolutionary look
that says I am in the world
to change the world

my lifetime
is to love to endure to suffer the music
to set its portrait
up as a sheet of the world
the most moving the most alive
Easter and bone
and Faust walking among the flowers of the world
and the child alive within the living woman, music of man,
and death holding my lifetime between great hands
the hands of enduring life

13

14   Käthe Kollwitz: *Run Over,* lithograph, 1910

15 Käthe Kollwitz: *Self-Portrait,* woodcut, 1924

that suffers the gifts and madness of full life, on earth, in our time,
and through my life, through my eyes, through my arms and hands
may give the face of this music in portrait waiting for
the unknown person
held in the two hands, you.

II

Woman as gates, saying:
"The process is after all like music,
like the development of a piece of music.
The fugues come back and
                                    again and again
interweave.
A theme may seem to have been put aside,
but it keeps returning—
the same thing modulated,
somewhat changed in form.
Usually richer.
And it is very good that this is so."

A woman pouring her opposites.
"After all there are happy things in life too.
Why do you show only the dark side?"
"I could not answer this. But I know—
In the beginning my impulse to know
the working life
                        had little to do with
pity or sympathy.
                        I simply felt
that the life of the workers was beautiful."

She said, "I am groping in the dark."

She said, "When the door opens, of sensuality,
then you will understand it too. The struggle begins.
Never again to be free of it,
often you will feel it to be your enemy.
Sometimes
you will almost suffocate,
such joy it brings."

Saying of her husband: "My wish
is to die after Karl.

I know no person who can love as he can,
with his whole soul.
Often this love has oppressed me;
I wanted to be free.
But often too it has made me
so terribly happy."

She said: "We rowed over to Carrara at dawn,
climbed up to the marble quarries
and rowed back at night. The drops of water
fell like glittering stars
from our oars."

She said: "As a matter of fact,
I believe
        that bisexuality
is almost a necessary factor
in artistic production; at any rate,
the tinge of masculinity within me
helped me
        in my work."

She said: "The only technique I can still manage.
It's hardly a technique at all, lithography.
In it
    only the essentials count."

A tight-lipped man in a restaurant last night
    saying to me:
"Kollwitz? She's too black-and-white."

III

Held among wars, watching
    all of them
    all these people
    weavers,
    Carmagnole

Looking at
    all of them
    death, the children
    patients in waiting-rooms
    famine

the street
the corpse with the baby
floating, on the dark river

A woman seeing
the violent, inexorable
movement of nakedness
and the confession of No
the confession of great weakness, war,
all streaming to one son killed, Peter;
even the son left living; repeated,
the father, the mother; the grandson
another Peter killed in another war; firestorm;
dark, light, as two hands.
this pole and that pole as the gates.

What would happen if one woman told the truth about her life?
The world would split open

IV   Song: The Calling-Up

Rumor, stir of ripeness
rising within this girl
sensual blossoming
of meaning, its light and form.

The birth-cry summoning
out of the male, the father
from the warm woman
a mother in response.

The word of death
calls up the fight with stone
wrestle with grief with time
from the material make
an art harder than bronze.

V   Self-Portrait

Mouth looking directly at you
eyes in their inwardness looking
directly at you
half light   half darkness

Käthe Kollwitz: *Chatting Women,* lithograph, 1933

woman, strong, German, young artist
flows into
wide sensual mouth meditating
looking right at you
eyes shadowed with brave hand
looking deep at you
flows into
wounded brave mouth
grieving and hooded eyes
alive, German, in her first War
flows into
strength of the worn face
a skein of lines
broods, flows into
mothers among the war graves
bent over death
facing the father
stubborn upon the field
flows into
the marks of her knowing—
Nie Wieder Krieg
repeated in the eyes
flows into
"Seedcorn must not be ground"
and the grooved cheek
lips drawn fine
the down-drawn grief
face of our age
flows into
Pieta, mother and
between her knees
life as her son in death
pouring from the sky of
one more war
flows into
face almost obliterated
hand over the mouth forever
hand over one eye now
the other great eye
closed

1971

21 | Käthe Kollwitz, 1935 (photographer unknown)

Paula Modersohn-Becker: *Portrait of Clara Rilke-Westhoff*, 1905

Diane Radycki
on
Adrienne Rich
on
Paula Modersohn-Becker

The autumn feels slowed down,
summer still holds on here, even the light
seems to last longer than it should
or maybe I'm using it to the thin edge.
The moon rolls in the air. I didn't want this child.

The moon rolls in the air. The *oo*'s and the *ll*'s hold on to the
sentence, just as Paula Becker holds on to the light of the fad-
ing summer, the season of fullness. She is full, in the final
months of pregnancy, between summer and fall, about to give
birth and about to die.

The mother who never encouraged her artist daughter
during her lifetime declared at Becker's death that now she
"understood." Shortly afterwards Becker's artist friends, who
ignored her during her eight years among them in Worpswede,
cleared out her studio and were amazed by her paintings. A
year later the poet Rainer Maria Rilke, who did not include
her in his monograph on the Worpswede artists (1903), was
still haunted by her untimely death and wrote his "Requiem
(for a Friend)" to purge the ghost.

The courage to appreciate Becker's life and work that her
family and friends gained from her death is dilatory, passive,
and gratuitous compared to the risks Becker took pursuing her

Becker with Otto Modersohn and Elsbeth
(his daughter from his first marriage), 1902-3

Becker in her Worpswede studio

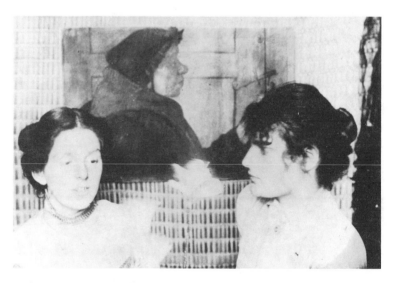

Becker with Clara Westhoff

Becker, about 1903

Paula Modersohn-Becker: *Self-Portrait*, 1903

work. Adrienne Rich reclaims the present tense for Becker and dares to speak in Becker's voice. Addressing her best friend, the sculptor Clara Westhoff, Becker reflects on the course of their lives, their friendship, and her pregnancy— which she knew would change her life (and we know ended it). It is this terrible foreknowledge that charges every sentence for us. Rich movingly voices Becker's plans for the future and her fear of dying. It is only with a great deal of conscious effort that we remind ourselves that Rich, not Becker, is speaking; but we are always aware that it is ourselves. not Westhoff, listening.

In empathy, in absolute identification with another woman who lived more than seventy years ago, Rich risks naming Becker's innermost feelings. Sometimes Rich proves to be uncannily accurate, saying almost word for word in 1975 what Becker did say, in letters just made available in Germany in 1979. Rich: "I didn't want this child. / You're the only one I've told. / I want a child maybe, someday, but not now." Becker (to her husband Modersohn): "Nor do I want a child by you, not *now.*" Rich: "Clara, our strength still lies / in the things we used to talk about: / . . . our old pledge against guilt." Becker: "So much has happened to me and I still don't feel guilty."

However, Rich does take a wrong direction in having Becker confide, "maybe I married Otto to fill up / my loneliness for you." While Becker did marry shortly after Westhoff, her engagement had taken place some eight months earlier. When this engagement became an open secret, Rilke abruptly abandoned the Worpswede house he had just rented and moved to Berlin. Then he unexpectedly married Westhoff in April. The emotional entanglement of Rilke with Becker will always be ripe for interpretation because there is a gap in his journals from the period immediately following Paula's engagement. Rilke scholarship suggests a different speaker for Rich's line: "Maybe I married Clara to fill up my loneliness for you."

Becker herself was a prolific writer, and many of her letters and journals were first published in 1920. Rich incorporates images from Becker's life as well as Becker's own words: "Marriage is lonelier than solitude." "Life and death take one another's hands." Rich also uses a phrase from Rilke's "Requiem," but with an important difference. Rilke says:

> But now I accuse: not Him [Modersohn] who took
>   you from yourself
> (I can't single him out, he's like them all)
> but in him I accuse all of them: Man.*

Rilke's "them" removes him from responsibility. Rich turns
Rilke's accusation on himself:

> he [Rilke] believes in women. But he feeds on us,
> like all of them. His whole life, his art
> is protected by women. Which of us could say that?
> Which of us, Clara, hasn't had to take that leap
> out beyond our being women
> to save our work? or is it to save ourselves?

Rilke ended his elegy with a cry to Becker's ghost to
"hear me, help me." Rich ends her poem with Becker appeal-
ing to Westhoff:

> ... Clara, I feel so full
> of work, the life I see ahead, and love
> for you, who of all people
> however badly I say this
> will hear all I say and cannot say.

Rilke is speaking for himself; Rich is speaking for Becker—but
not one to one, not to Clara Westhoff, but to us. In lines
finely constructed to give both general and specific meaning
to "full" and "love," and with a pull from beyond the grave,
Rich asks for the understanding Becker did not have during
her life. We are the ones privy to what she "cannot say."

I have translated Becker's writings and am stunned by
Rich's immediate and intimate voicing of Becker's interior
life. And her choice of having Becker speak to her closest
friend effectively gives Becker back to women. After Becker's
death men made monuments to her. The sculptor Bernhard
Hoetger erected a statue of a dying mother on the painter's
grave. While his monument is reasonably modest and pleasant,
it is ultimately a sexist sentimentality and in remarkable contrast to Becker's own desire (which was briefly carried out):
"At the head of my grave perhaps two small junipers; in the
center a small black wooden plaque with my name—no dates
or words." Since 1909 the last word on Becker has been Rilke's. By using the first person, Rich now allows Becker that
word. Rich takes her from the ferocious finality of death,
elegy, monument, and opens up her life again. She challenges
us to the impossible dialogue with the voices of women un-
heard in their lifetimes.

Diane Radycki

*Adrienne Rich generously supplied me with her and Lilly Engler's
unpublished translation of Rilke's "Requiem." Frau Becker's state-
ments and the Worpswede artists' reaction were told to me by the
Modersohn family and Siegrid Weltge.

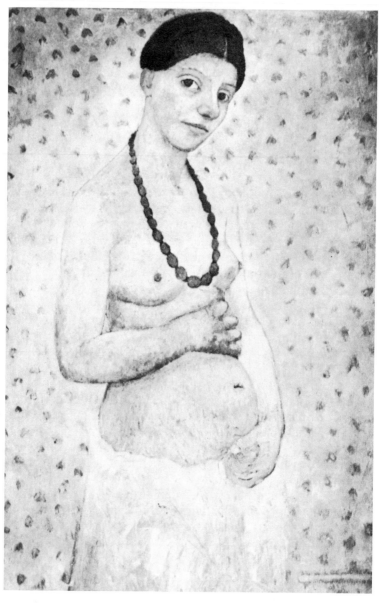

Paula Modersohn-Becker: *Self-Portrait on her Sixth Wedding Anniversary*, 1906. Actually painted in the year before she became pregnant and before her sixth anniversary.

Paula Becker to Clara Westhoff

by Adrienne Rich

Paula Becker 1876-1907
Clara Westhoff 1878-1954

became friends at Worpswede, an artists' colony near Bremen, Germany, summer 1899. In January 1900, spent a half-year together in Paris, where Paula painted and Clara studied sculpture with Rodin. In August they returned to Worpswede, and spent the next winter together in Berlin. In 1901, Clara married the poet Rainer Maria Rilke; soon after, Paula married the painter Otto Modersohn. She died in a hemorrhage after childbirth, murmuring, *What a pity!*

The autumn feels slowed down,
summer still holds on here, even the light
seems to last longer than it should
or maybe I'm using it to the thin edge.
The moon rolls in the air. I didn't want this child.
You're the only one I've told.
I want a child maybe, someday, but not now.
Otto has a calm, complacent way
of following me with his eyes, as if to say
Soon you'll have your hands full!
And yes, I will; this child will be mine
not his, the failures, if I fail
will all be mine. We're not good, Clara,
at learning to prevent these things,
and once we have a child, it *is* ours.
But lately, I feel beyond Otto or anyone.
I know now the kind of work I have to do.
It takes such energy! I have the feeling I'm
moving somewhere, patiently, impatiently,
in my loneliness. I'm looking everywhere in nature
for new forms, old forms in new places,
the planes of an antique mouth, let's say, among the leaves.

I know and do not know
what I am searching for.
Remember those months in the studio together,
you up to your strong forearms in wet clay,
I trying to make something of the strange impressions
assailing me—the Japanese
flowers and birds on silk, the drunks
sheltering in the Louvre, that river-light,
those faces. . . . Did we know exactly
why we were there? Paris unnerved you,
you found it too much, yet you went on
with your work . . . and later we met there again,
both married then, and I thought you and Rilke
both seemed unnerved. I felt a kind of joylessness
between you. Of course he and I
have had our difficulties. Maybe I was jealous
of him, to begin with, taking you from me,
maybe I married Otto to fill up
my loneliness for you.
Rainer, of course, *knows* more than Otto knows,
he believes in women. But he feeds on us,
like all of them. His whole life, his art
is protected by women. Which of us could say that?
Which of us, Clara, hasn't had to take that leap
out beyond our being women
to save our work? or is it to save ourselves?
Marriage is lonelier than solitude.
Do you know: I was dreaming I had died
giving birth to the child.
I couldn't paint or speak or even move.
My child—I think—survived me. But what was funny
in the dream was, Rainer had written my requiem—
a long, beautiful poem, and calling me his friend.
I was *your* friend
but in the dream you didn't say a word.
In the dream his poem was like a letter
to someone who has no right
to be there but must be treated gently, like a guest
who comes on the wrong day. Clara, why don't I dream of you?
That photo of the two of us—I have it still,
you and I looking hard into each other
and my painting behind us. How we used to work
side by side! And how I've worked since then
trying to create according to our plan
that we'd bring, against all odds, our full power

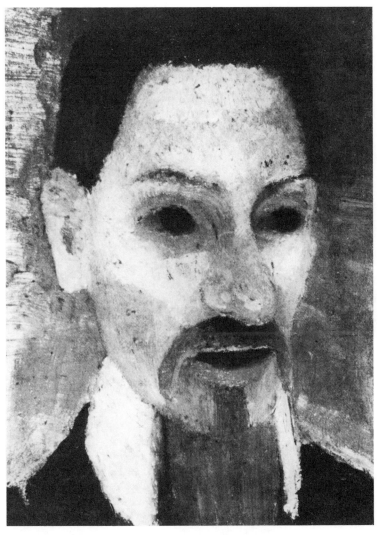

33 | Paula Modersohn-Becker: *Portrait of Rainer Maria Rilke*, 1905

34 | Paula Modersohn-Becker: *Portrait of Otto Modersohn*

to every subject. Hold back nothing
because we were women. Clara, our strength still lies
in the things we used to talk about:
how life and death take one another's hands,
the struggle for truth, our old pledge against guilt.
And now I feel dawn and the coming day.
I love waking in my studio, seeing my pictures
come alive in the light. Sometimes I feel
it is myself that kicks inside me,
myself I must give suck to, love . . .
I wish we could have done this for each other
all our lives, but we can't . . .
They say a pregnant woman
dreams of her own death. But life and death
take one another's hands. Clara, I feel so full
of work, the life I see ahead, and love
for you, who of all people
however badly I say this
will hear all I say and cannot say.

1975-1976

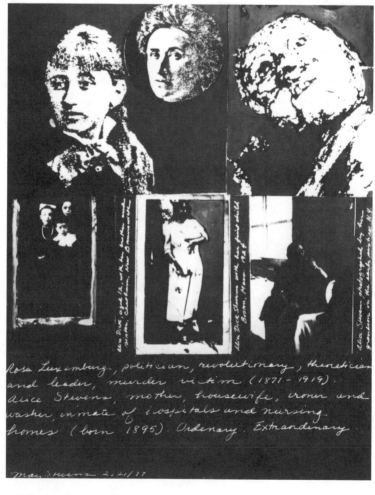

Rosa Luxemburg, politician, revolutionary, theoretician and leader, murder victim (1871 - 1919). Alice Stevens, mother, housewife, ironer and washer, inmate of hospitals and nursing homes (born 1895). Ordinary. Extraordinary.

May Stevens 2.21.77

All illustrations in this section are from May Stevens'
artist's book *Ordinary, Extraordinary*.

May Stevens
on
Jane Cooper
on
Rosa Luxemburg

With the publication of "Threads: Rosa Luxemburg from Prison," Jane Cooper joins Muriel Rukeyser and Adrienne Rich in writing through the persona of a self-realized woman who lived in the early part of our century. Rich in "Paula Becker to Clara Westhoff" and Rukeyser in "Käthe Kollwitz" chose artists whose lives are inseparable from historical events while exemplifying historical limitations: Paula Becker bringing post-impressionism to North German art circles, suffering the constriction marriage imposes on the talent-burdened woman artist, and dying after childbirth in a time-bound not-now-necessary way; Käthe Kollwitz living her life as an artist informed by socialist understanding, emotionally responding to the poverty around her in Berlin between the wars, and suffering the loss of first a son, then a grandson, to those wars. Rosa Luxemburg not only suffered loss and deprivation from the same war that took Kollwitz' son, she was imprisoned and eventually killed for her leadership in shaping political forces intended to correct that poverty and that war. Astonishingly, in Luxemburg, as Jane Cooper shows, political power lived alongside a nature as sensitive to esthetic considerations as Becker's or Kollwitz'.

Cooper's source, Rosa's letters to Sonya Liebknecht, whose husband was imprisoned on the same charges, scarcely records the degradation of imprisonment. Instead they attempt to comfort the younger woman, widowed by separation, left to spend her young woman's vitality in single parenting and the bewilderment of those who undergo the effects of political punishment without being able to draw from it the same sustenance and meaning as the involved one, as Rosa herself, as shaper and maker could.

What Cooper has done in her long three-part poem is to trace the changes that overtake the revolutionary leader in a year's time, shut away from her work and her comrades. It is May 23, 1917, and Rosa is reading in the natural sciences and watching the songbirds take care of their family dramas and beetles and butterflies cope with daily disasters. The section ends:

38

What is the meaning of it all? What is the meaning
of young weeds tufted in the prison wall? young poplar shoots?
underground passages of wasp and wild bee
I try not to shake when I walk? ant highways
straight as the Roman?

In the middle section, moved now from her cell in Wronke to a new one in Breslau, Rosa must integrate the death of
a friend killed at the front. She hallucinates:

. . . I read
in an intoxication of calm. I look up
to smile at Hans as if he stood in the door.
These forces, these cataclysms that would sweep us away,
we have to accept them
as subjects of study, data for exploration

The solution of this active woman confined to the pas-
sivity of small cell and prison yard, while great events *that
need her* take place just beyond her, is to cool her thoughts
in the vastness of the migration of birds:

Eagles, falcons, hawks, owls   All the birds of prey
flying to Egypt   Bird migrations
always a puzzle to me
over the blue Mediterranean

. . .
Flying with them   so many that the sky floods dark:
nightingales; larks, golden-crested wrens
A cloud of songbirds
Thousands of natural victims
without fear

. . .
All of them flying toward a common goal

In the final section, Rosa's petition for release has been
rejected:

It seems I am going to stay here
till we have conquered the whole world

It is spring again; Sonya must report the spring.

Darling, the earth is faithful, the one thing
fresh but yet faithful. Be my eyes for me,
let me see all you see

. . .
Sonya, for my sake
please go to the Botanical Gardens,
let me hear all you hear,
for over and above the outcome of the Battle of Cambrai,
this really seems to me
the most important issue of the day

And the woman in the cell has moved from

. . . These are the chosen tracks
down which the future will break forth. If only the war lasts. . . .

to the tenderness of one almost flayed. Almost a year after
the poem's starting point, she writes:

> . . . Strange
> how most people see nothing, most people
> feel the earth firm under their feet when it is
> flaming
> *whereas my concern for organic nature is by now almost morbid in its*
> *intensity*

What Jane Cooper has done is turn prose into poetry
through her careful constructions and juxtapositions. Com-
paring these pages with the actual letters Luxemburg wrote,
one sees the fine ear of the poet at work, tuning Rosa's words
and creating through the necessary ellipses the verbal shocks
and images that make Rosa's voice carry across the intervening
sixty years. It is through a synchronization of sensibilities that
we can hear Rosa's voice. It is possible, of course, that this
Rosa has been fashioned for our time—to meet our needs.
Cooper has found an essential sustaining core in Luxemburg's
spirit upon which her political commitment was based: the
necessity of being connected to life in all its striving forms:

> *It's no use telling myself I am not responsible for all the hungry*
> *little larks in the world. Logic does not help*
> Never mind, we shall live   shall live
> through grand events
> Have patience
> Thus passing out of my cell in all directions
> are fine threads connecting me
> with thousands of birds and beasts
> You too, Sonitchka, are one of this urgent company
> to which my whole self throbs, responsive
> . . .
> not Flanders alone has become the beloved
> but all nature   beyond even
> the radiant skin
> of the globe

As an artist involved in my own work with what Rosa
said and what she did and how she looked, I feel particularly
close to this poem. I also know nothing can take the place of
the texts that carry Rosa's voice in its fullest and most direct
explication of a vision not yet fully understood nor acted
upon. *Threads* suggests to the reader the quality of that
vision. To those familiar with Luxemburg's contributions to
political theory, Jane Cooper's poem proposes the essential
female character of her mind, a mind so careful in its bril-
liance that no lark should be left unfed.

Threads:
Rosa Luxemburg from Prison
by Jane Cooper

I. *Wronke,* Spring 1917

> *You ask what I am reading. Natural science for the most part;*
> *I am studying the distribution of plants and animals.*

A huge white poplar half fills the prison garden.
All the songbirds love that tree best. The young leaves
sticky all over with a white down
shine in the sun like flowers!
But by now the small birds
(May 23rd) are much too busy to sing.
Hens keep their nests, cocks with their beaks full
streak back and forth. Yesterday—
yes, for the first time in almost three weeks
I caught the *zeezeebey!* of a blue tit
shrilling over the wall.
At fourteen I was proud, I pitied my mother
for telling me Solomon understood the gossip of birds.
Now I'm like Solomon, that quick *zeezeebey!*
roused me to the sorrows of bird life

I must be out of sorts, just now I was reading
how in the name of scientific agriculture
we've drained the swamps, chopped down brushwood and stumps,
cleared away leaves,
while civilized men (according to Professor Sieber)

drove the Redskins from their feeding grounds
in North America

And they made you talk to Karl
through a grating?
I remember in Warsaw
I was on hunger strike, I could barely stand.
My brother came to see me. They propped me in a cage,
a cage within a cage. (I gripped with both hands
to hold myself upright.) From the outer wires
he peered across as at a zoo. *Where are you?* he asked,
again and again brushing away the tears that clouded his glasses

But you make too much of my "equanimity," Sonya.
It is simply my way
when I suffer not to utter a word

Sonyusha, I know I can say this to you, my darling—
You will not promptly accuse me
of treason against socialism. Suppose I am really
not a human being at all but some bird or beast?
I walk up and down my scrap of prison garden
—I'm alone in a field where the grass is humming with bees—
and I feel more at home
than at a party congress. Of course I always
mean to die at my post, in a street fight
or prison. But my first self
belongs to the tomtits more than our comrades.

Still, nature is cruel, not a refuge,
and—you won't mind?—I have to laugh
a little when you ask me, *How can men dare*
judge you and Karl? My little bird,
given the totality of vital forms
through twenty thousand years of civilization,
that's not a reasonable question! Why are there blue tits?
Zeezeebey! but I'm awfully glad there are.
We live in the painfulest moment of evolution,
the very chapter of change, and you have to ask,
What is the meaning of it all? Listen,
one day I found a beetle stunned on its back,
its legs gnawed to stumps by ants; another day
I clambered to free a peacock butterfly
battering half dead inside our bathroom pane.

I swear to you, let me once get out of prison and I shall hunt and disperse your company of singing toads with trumpets, whips and bloodhounds . . . . see to it that you remain a human being. To be human is the main thing, and that means to be strong and clear and of good cheer in spite and because of everything, for tears are the preoccupation of weakness. To be human means throwing one's life 'on the scales of destiny' if need be, to be joyful for every fine day and every beautiful cloud — oh I can't write you any recipes how to be human, I only know how to be human and you used to know it when we walked for a few hours in the fields outside Berlin and watched the red sunset over the corn The world is so beautiful in spite of all the misery and would be even more beautiful if there were no half-wits and cowards in it.
Wronke 28 December 1916   Rosa Luxemburg

43   May Stevens

Locked up myself after six, I lean on the sill.
The sky's like iron, a heavy rain falls, the nightingale
sings in the sycamore as if possessed.
What is the meaning of it all? What is the meaning
of young weeds tufted in the prison wall? young poplar shoots?
underground passages of wasp and wild bee
I try not to shake when I walk? ant highways
straight as the Roman? The wall stones shine with wet,
reddish, bluish—a comfort even on
color-starved winter days—gray and resurgent green

II.   *Breslau,* November-December 1917

I had a vision of all the splendor of war!

Hans is killed
   Now twilight begins at four
N "broke the news"
    Over the great paved courtyard
     hundreds of rooks fly by with a rowing stroke
Such a parade of grief! Why can't friends understand
I need solitude to consider? Why not tell me
quickly, briefly, simply
so as not to cheapen
    Their homecoming caw,
     throaty and muted, is so different from their
     sharp morning caw after food. As if metal balls,
     tossed from one to the other, high in the air,
     tinkled exchanging the day's news
my last two letters
addressed to a dead man
    stolen greetings
    passed between me and the rooks
    here in the darkening yard
I'm allowed so few letters. But from now on, Sonitchka,
I can talk to you again—I mean on paper—
just as before

If only I could send you
like a starry cloak
the confident joy I feel. I lie awake
in black wrappings of boredom, unfreedom and cold.
A distant train hoots. Now there's the squeak

44

of damp gravel under the desolate boot
of the midnight guard, who coughs. It becomes a song.
My cell trembles. I'm lying in a field streaked with light.
How can that be? My heart beats. Life itself,
the riddle, becomes the key to the riddle. Even this war,
this huge asylum, this casual misery
in which we dream, this too must be transformed
into something meant, heroic. Like an elemental force,
some flood or hurricane, like an eclipse of the sun,
absurd to judge it! These are the chosen tracks
down which the future will break forth. If only the war lasts. . . .
Meanwhile, I'm deep in geology.
You may find that dry, but it opens up
the vastest conception of nature, the most unified view
of any science. I read
in an intoxication of calm. I look up
to smile at Hans as if he stood in the door.
These forces, these cataclysms that would sweep us away,
we have to accept them
as subjects of study, data for exploration

Eagles, falcons, hawks, owls   All the birds of prey
flying to Egypt   Bird migrations
always a puzzle to me
over the blue Mediterranean
        From Rumania: war trophies
        A hundred head of buffalo
        in Breslau alone
        These beasts, stronger than oxen
        Their horns recurved
        over a skull flat as a sheep's
        Black hide   Huge, soft eyes
Flying with them   so many that the sky floods dark:
nightingales, larks, golden-crested wrens
A cloud of songbirds
Thousands of natural victims
without fear
        Rough army drays
        drawn up in the courtyard where I take my walks
        the load: haversacks, old army tunics, shirts
        darkened, soaked with blood
        Brought here from the front
        for the women prisoners to mend
All of them flying toward a common goal:
to drop half dead

May Stevens

beside the Nile
and sort themselves into territories and species
> Today a towering dray
> dragged by a team of freshly broken beasts
> The soldier-driver
> beating and beating with the butt of his whip
> Even our woman gatekeeper protesting
> One ripped and bleeding
> its stiff hide torn
> the look on its black face like a weeping child's
> The rest of the team
> half dead   standing while the dray was emptied at last
> perfectly still

Reading
how on the long flight south larger birds
often carry the small   Reading:
cranes
sighted in amazing numbers along the coast
with a twittering freight
of songbirds on their backs
> Eyes
> of the bleeding   My own dark
> handsomely photographed eyes
> Tears / negative
> Tears / negative
> Tears / negative   of my own face dead
> skull beaten in and
> drowned

The suffering of a dearly loved brother could hardly have affected me
more profoundly
As if all the birds declared
> Brother! I am one with you
a "truce of God!"
> one with your pain, your helplessness, your longing
> one with you in my helplessness

> > The music of the songbirds
> > in the flowery meadows of Rumania
> > The mythical herdsman's call

Meanwhile the women prisoners were jostling one another as they
busily unloaded the dray and carried the heavy sacks into the adminis-
tration building. The driver, hands in his pockets, was striding up and
down the courtyard smiling to himself as he whistled a popular air. I
had a vision of all the splendor of war!

III. *Breslau,* Spring 1918

I am so looking forward to spring. It is the only thing one never gets tired of.

My window looks on the red brick wall
of the men's prison
           My petition for release
           has been rejected
Just the crests of trees
blur above the roofs of the lunatic asylum
           My petition   even for a brief furlough
           rejected
Here, unfortunately, that is all one can see
over the high brick wall
           It seems I am going to stay here
           till we have conquered the whole world

This lovely world! If only we could walk through it, talk
freely together, weep over it. Sonyusha,
whenever I don't hear from you, I fear you're driven,
whipped by the winds of your loneliness,
helpless as a young leaf. The days grow long,
the clouds rush by. Our chalky soil,
which doesn't yet show it's been planted,
streams with changing lights. Get out as much as you can.
Darling, the earth is faithful, the one thing
fresh but yet faithful. Be my eyes for me,
let me see all you see

This March seems fateful. Strange, to hear them singing
far off from the grounds of the lunatic asylum:
nightingales, wrynecks, golden orioles
(that "Whitsun bird"), never heard till April here,
never heard till May   laughing and
fluting in the
pale gray light
before dawn
What is the reason for this premature migration?
Is it meant for Berlin too?
Sonya, for my sake
please go to the Botanical Gardens,
let me hear all you hear,

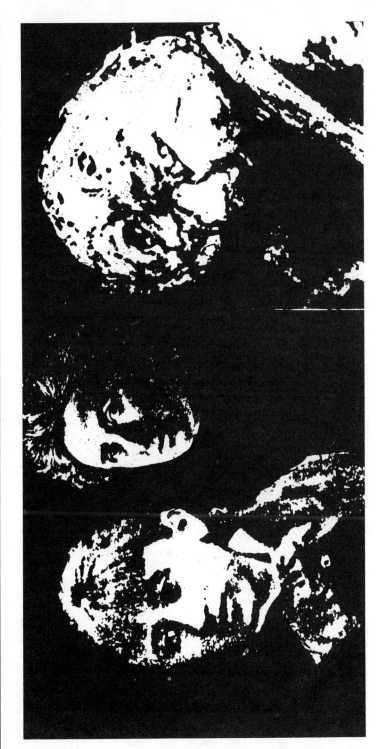

May Stevens: *Three Images of Rosa Luxemburg*

Luxemburg i

May Stevens

for over and above the outcome of the Battle of Cambrai,
this really seems to me
the most important issue of the day

May 12th. Fragments of the established world
flame and submerge, they tear away. Day by day
we witness fresh catastrophes   Strange
how most people see nothing, most people
feel the earth firm under their feet when it is
flaming
whereas my concern for organic nature is by now almost morbid in its
intensity
Dusk: down below in the court
a young crested lark is running with short steps,
fluttering up and piping. I listen for the soft *hweet! hweet!*
of the parent birds seeking food. It makes me ill
to see such suffering
            I feel how you   must be suffering
and I can do nothing to help
My buffaloes still come, my foolish starling
is missing
            suffering because you can't "live"
sparrows and pigeons
follow me about like dogs
for a crumb
It's no use telling myself I am not responsible for all the hungry
little larks in the world. Logic does not help
            Never mind, we shall live   shall live
            through grand events
            Have patience
Thus passing out of my cell in all directions
are fine threads connecting me
with thousands of birds and beasts
            You too, Sonitchka, are one of this urgent company
            to which my whole self throbs, responsive
Write soon. Please tell me how Karl is.
Perhaps Pfemfert can find you *The Flax Field*
by Streuvels. For these Flemish authors
not Flanders alone has become the beloved
but all nature   beyond even
the radiant skin
of the globe.

Rosa Luxemburg: *Her Eyes*

Rosa Luxemburg attending the Congress of the Second Inter
national in Amsterdam, 1904. Detail from *One Plus or Minus One*,
installation at the New Museum of Contemporary Art, New York
City, 1988

Biographical Notes

Lucy Lippard is a writer and activist who lives in New York and Boulder, Colorado. Her book of feminist essays on women's art, *From the Center* (NY: Dutton, 1976), established a new feminist criticism. Her most recent book is *Mixed Blessings: Contemporary Art and the Cross-Cultural Process* (NY: Pantheon, 1990).

Martha Kearns is an art historian, humanities educator, author and critic. Her works include *Käthe Kollwitz: Woman and Artist*, the definitive biography of the artist in English; poetry, children's short stories, drama, essays; and art, drama and literary criticism.

Muriel Rukeyser (1913-1980), born in New York City, wrote fourteen books of poetry, five prose works, children's books, at least two plays, essays, biographies of scientists, and several volumes of translations. Her first volume of poems appeared in 1935; throughout her life she spoke with a brave, strong voice—her poetry interweaving politics and personal life. Her concerns were the individual and his/her confrontation with a constantly changing world. She was a past president of P.E.N.—Poets, Playwrights, Essayists, Editors, and Novelists. She received numerous awards and prizes—the Shelley Memorial Award, a Guggenheim Fellowship, and the Copernicus Award among them. She was honored in 1979 at the *New York Quarterly* Poetry Day for "her outstanding contribution to contemporary poetry."

Käthe Kollwitz (1867-1945), a graphic artist and sculptor who lived in Berlin, is particularly well known for her superb woodcuts and lithographs. As the 1899 recipient of the Gold Medal, Germany's highest award for artistic achievement, Kollwitz became the most recognized woman artist in Europe. This distinction also made her the token female in art organizations, institutions, and exhibitions, and in professional and social clubs. An ardent socialist and pacifist, she reflected political oppression and private suffering in her art. Many of her works portray and condemn the misery and hunger of the poor, and her posters became tools of political education, calling attention to the issues of abortion, hunger, alcoholism, worker safety, and child welfare. Because of the political content of her work, she lost her position as director of the graphic arts department of the Berlin Academy in 1932, with the rise of the Nazi party. Kollwitz lived the physically vigorous life of an average working woman, spending the mornings in her studio and attending to her two sons, Hans and Peter, and her husband, Karl, a doctor who served the working-class community of their northeast Berlin neighborhood. Although in her work she was fearless, in her personal life she was known for her reserve and shyness. She did not often disclose her feelings and opinions even to members of her own family. Her life was governed by the personal philosophy she had learned from her grandfather: "One's life is not important; one's work is."

Diane Radycki is a writer, art historian, and photographer who spent 1989-90 in Germany as a Fulbright Fellow. She translated and annotated *The Letters and Journals of Paula Modersohn-Becker*. Radycki is currently a PhD candidate at Harvard.

Adrienne Rich has published some fourteen books of poems, including *The Dream of a Common Language* (1978) and *Time's Power: Poems 1985-1988*, and several prose works, including *On Lies, Secrets, and Silence: Selected Prose 1966-1978*, and *Blood, Bread, and Poetry: Selected Prose 1979-1986*. She has read her poems and lectured on feminist issues at universities here and abroad. She has taught writing and women's studies at Swarthmore, Columbia, the City College of New York, Brandeis and Rutgers. She received an honorary Litt.D. from Smith College in 1979, was awarded the first annual Ruth Lilly Poetry Prize and the Brandeis University Creative Arts Medal. She is a lesbian/feminist, active in the women's movement, and makes her home in California.

Paula Modersohn-Becker (1876-1907), like Kollwitz, came of a non-artistic background—a recent phenomenon in the history of women artists. Her training in London and Berlin in the 1890s was in traditional academic styles. In 1898 she settled in Worpswede, an artists' colony near Bremen, and three years later she married the landscape painter Otto Modersohn. Unlike the other Worpswede artists, she frequently traveled to Paris. She developed her own simplified, monumental forms and a heavy, rich palette. Her decision to take leave of her husband in order to live and work in Paris was undermined by both family and friends (except for the poet Rainer Maria Rilke and the sculptor Clara Westhoff). Pregnant, she returned to Germany with her husband and died three weeks after giving birth to her first child. She was a prolific artist, obsessed with painting, and produced more than 400 works in her 31 years. Before any other German artist, she reached the threshold of modernism.

May Stevens is a New York painter. Her essay "My Work and My Working-Class Father" was published in *Working It Out: 23 Women Writers, Artists, Scientists, and Scholars Talk About Their Lives and*

Work, edited by Sara Ruddick and Pamela Daniels (1977). She showed *One Plus or Minus One*, a major installation, in the Main Gallery of the New Museum of Contemporary Art, New York, in 1988, and later the same year at the Orchard Gallery in Derry, Northern Ireland. A monograph on the *Ordinary, Extraordinary* Series was published in 1988 under the title *Rosa Alice*.

Jane Cooper is the author of three books of poems, *The Weather of Six Mornings*, which was the Lamont Selection of the Academy of American Poets for 1968, *Maps and Windows*, and *Scaffolding: New and Selected Poems*, which won the Maurice English Poetry Award in 1985. Other honors have included a Shelley Award from the Poetry Society of America, and fellowships from the Guggenheim Foundation, the Ingram Merrill Foundation, the National Endowment for the Arts, and the Bunting Institute of Radcliffe College. She taught for many years at Sarah Lawrence College. "Threads" was first published as a chapbook and sold for the benefit of an anti-nuclear group of the War Resisters League. The poem is based on Rosa Luxemburg's *Prison Letters* to Sophie Liebknecht, the wife of her friend and co-revolutionary Karl Liebknecht. Together Rosa Luxemburg and Karl Liebnecht founded the Spartacus League and later opposed the Kaiser's war policy, and they spent almost the whole of World War I as political prisoners in (different) German cities. They were released a few days before the Armistice, only to be picked up again in early 1919 by government authorities, interrogated, and killed. The young doctor Hans Dieffenbach, mentioned in Part II of "Threads," was killed at the front.

Rosa Luxemburg was born in 1871 to a well-off family in Zamosc, Poland, one of the centers of Jewish life in Eastern Europe. As a small child she suffered from a hip disease that, wrongly diagnosed, left her with a permanent limp. She wrote poetry, painted, and sang German lieder. All her life she had an intense interest in nature and the natural sciences. In 1889 she left Poland to study philosophy and law at the University of Zurich. After receiving her doctorate in political science, she emigrated to Germany, where she joined the Social Democratic Party. From that time until her assassination in January of 1919, she was one of the foremost intellectual and political leaders in the Marxist world. She lectured all over Germany; she wrote hundreds of articles and edited *Rote Fahne*, the organ of the revolutionary Spartacus League, which she founded with Karl Liebknecht; and she debated with every major Marxist theoretician of the age, including Lenin. Her masterwork was *The Accumulation of Capital*. She was imprisoned several times for her radical politics and activism, and when she was assassinated her skull was smashed with a rifle butt and her body thrown into a Berlin canal. She was 47 years old. In a letter she wrote: "To be human is the main thing." She gave her life for that belief.

Illustrations

Cover: Carol Winer
Original design and typography: Lucinda Cisler
Second printing typography: Barbara Bergeron